Endurance

By Brian Bucks

Bucks Enterprises – Services and Training, INC.
90444 County Road H
Mitchell, NE. 69357

ISBN: 0692624309
ISBN-13: 978-0692624302

Printed in the U.S.A.
First Printing – February 2016

Cover photograph © 2015 Brian Bucks
Image of Spring Creek in the Black Hills of South Dakota.

DEDICATION

I dedicate this book to Colleen, my wife. She has shown me true love. Together, with God's mercy and grace, we have stayed together through horrible times and good times. To better days.

CONTENTS

Endurance

PREFACE

At first I wasn't going to include a preface and just let the poems speak for themselves. I changed my mind as I looked at the proof copy.

A book of poems isn't what I envisioned as my first book, especially on some of the topics included. Some of the topics are uncomfortable, languish on the periphery of life, and cause great harm to the soul. At my current place in life I am driven in my soul to be raw and real about this journey of life. Courage and vulnerability are important and deserve a voice. If I silence my voice out of fear I become less than human, succumbing to shame.

What captures me with poetry is the expression of the complexity of being human stripped to a raw form. Courage is required at times to speak clearly about topics we tend as a society to avoid. *Endurance* is about a journey. A journey that includes poems about observations of life that captured my attention; and poems about overcoming trauma and abuse.

In taking a creative writing course at the local community college, Western Nebraska Community College, I rediscovered a voice in writing that had been lost decades ago. I found moments where words spilled out covering journal pages. In the process I discovered the bulk of my writing actually falls into the free verse poetry category. As several genres were explored in the class I thrived in the poetry portion. The bulk of these poems were written in the past year.

Finally, I also want to be clear that many of the poems are about wrestling with God. Poems about the journey to new depths of intimacy with God in the midst of the reality of the messiness of life. Life isn't without ugly struggles, often those around us and society don't know how to respond. Their response or lack of response isn't a fair representation or interpretation of who God is or His love for the person in those dark places of the soul. You are not alone, He is with you.

So this book is dedicated to the courageous ones who will wrestle with God, not settling for the "pat" answers, formulas, or quick fixes. Endurance is developed in wrestling with God in those places that resist exposure; and builds muscle and character as you overcome while pushing into the resistance. Be encouraged in the place of your wrestling with God, seasons change and hope

returns.

Brian Bucks
February 2016
Western Nebraska

Endurance

They walked on the path.
He used a cane.
Almost leaning on each other, a bent together that held them up.
In their eighth decade, pasty white skin of a full life.
All bundled up against the light wind.
They are alive; holding hands, unashamed to be seen.
Arouses hope in soul, love hasn't grown cold.
Slowly they walk.

Fascinates me as others just walk by.
I slowdown as drive past soaking them in.
They have no idea of hope that stirs deep within.
Peacefulness as they walk, it oozes out.
If slow for a moment can enter their moment.

Joy in life, not about material things.
Joy in being with the one you love.
Joy in enduring the struggles and trials together.
Joy in the moments still have together.
Joy in bodies still able to walk together.
Joy in hope for today and still being known.
Joy in sharing life and love with lover, best friend.

Bask

In happy moments bask,
   Joy unmasked.
Revel in goodness,
   Celebrate and bless.
Caress lips of lover,
   Linger there, hover.
Gates open wide,
   In warm embrace abide.
Close cherished moments slip,
   Life severs and rips
Tears and sutures of day to day,
   Takes its toll on human clay.
Love pull me in close,
   Drug me with one more dose.
Bound and tethered,
   Velcro'd® together,
Souls lift,
   Each other's gift.
Time sifts,
   Life shifts.
Peaceful rest settles upon,
   All distance gone.

Courageous and Bold

Broken places, sorrow filled faces.
Expectations dashed, dumped in the trash.
Years of heartbreak consume the space.
Can we begin again, be so brash.

Story's familiar, not that peculiar.
One thought this, the other thought that.
Two people that clash, separated so far.
Deceived about this, can't clear the bar.

Caught by surprise, no more disguise.
Ambivalent moment between new and old.
Truth to be told, nor more lies.
One must be courageous and bold.

Unsleep

Fresh honest words strikes old wound.
Taken back to a place without a face.
My wound is real, how does it heal?
Not enough, try harder never worked.
What do I do with what I feel?
Emotions stuck within my soul.
Constricted throat, tightness of chest.
"Double-down," "micromanage" never enter into rest.

Taken away to another time, replace the thought.
Sounds of surf, rhythm of waves.
Soothes my soul, but still not whole.
So much energy, so much work.
Freedom is an inner place, a contented space.
Haunted places in the mind wakes me up way before dawn.
Something wants set free so I can become the congruent me.
Process thoughts and words that sting.
Sting has nothing to do with my wedding ring.
Wound came long before she was ever in my life, my wife.

Turbulence of crashing waves softly push up the sand.
Foam and froth, oh so soft.
Calms my mind, draws me out from inner place.
Lost in time and space.
Learned not to fight not being able to sleep.

Just get up without a peep, press into new place of unsleep.
There are no answers in moment just be real and honor self.
This is TRUE and is okay, won't always be a place I stay.
There is a day where salve applied and just a scar, a visible mar.
Peace crashes in waves, made whole in soul.

Spring's Delay

Meadow lark softly sings,
        Snow drifting down.
Pheasant's cry rings,
        Ground covered in white gown.

Air is cold,
        Sky is gray.
Winter is old,
        Blustery day.

No Luggage to Stow

The tick of the clock,
      Waves gently splash the dock.
Oceans away,
      In my mind today.
Longing of heart,
      New course to chart.
Voyage begins,
      Left luggage and sins.
No luggage to stow,
      Just walk aboard, let's go.
Like fleeing dissident,
      New country of residence.
Escape quickly, just flee,
      Grateful and pray on bended knee.

Trainer's Derogatory Words

Little did he know the words he used,
   Exposed his heart and what he viewed.
A snippet of this laid bare his thoughts,
   The emotion it wrought.

An internal cringe he couldn't see,
   Derogatory in story about who she would be.
If he heard his own voice,
   Sorrow would be his only choice.

Humor at expense of girls he loved,
   His own flesh and blood.
A type of abuse that starts in his mind,
   What love will they find.

Sexist would shock him,
   Yet flows over the brim.
Disbelief at called a chauvinist pig,
   Yet that's what it is with each subtle dig.

Intimacy

Intimacy, intimacy says hey look at me,
     In reality it isn't the key.
Anything less than oneness with Him,
     No matter the label, is a fleshly fantasy.
Intimacy can become just a word,
     A way to manage instead of True Love.
So easy to get lost in familiar trappings each day,
     One turn of the head and disconnection will be.
Locking my eyes in my Lover's gaze,
     IN TO ME He sees.
Mutual gaze, He into me and me into He,
     Love in a gaze, mercy will be.

Primal

Wild
Primal
Earthy
    Free
    Passionate
    Fierce
        Loyal
        Honoring
        Faithful
            Complete
            Whole
            Unified

Oneness

Bliss,
        The sweetest kiss.
Always there,
        Have I cared.
Two are bound,
        Love expounds.
Lost is found,
        Grace abounds.
Enter in,
        No power of sin.
Numb,
        Is dumb.
Don't push away,
        Don't betray.
Enter the fray,
        Stay engaged.
Push through the gate,
        Enter in.
Raw,
        Pain thaws.
Burned within,
        Seared by sin.
Merged,
        Passions surge.
Always with me,
        Presence sets free.
State of being,
        Not a place.
To see Your face,
        No more making my case.

Broken

Land of formulas is gone.
Time to stand naked, open before Him.

Exposure of truth.
Sears the heart.

Broken and busted I come.
Giving myself away.

No more sin or barrier between.
No more squirming or running away.

Honesty, truth, and love.
I give myself to You.

Nothing more or left to give.
The point of the journey is this.

Not my efforts, works, or things.
Just me and You with nothing in between.

You desire nothing more than me.
And I lovingly give myself back to You.

Dark Years

Part I

One day,
      One event.
Casts a shadow,
      Dims the light.

Seeds of thoughts,
      Planted deep.
Feeds on shame,
      Memories rent.

Darkness grows,
      Fears are fed.
Emotions numb,
      Soul is dead.

Day after day,
      Week to week.
Year to year,
      Fear is fed.

At the altar of shame,
      Hope is lost.
Wandering now,
      Depths of pain.

Year after year,
      Has love failed?
Wounded and scarred,
      Ugly and marred.

Soul is scuffed,
        Mind is tough.
Set to believe,
        My lies about me.

Part II

Yet love comes quickly,
        Violently.
Is the rescue of me,
        World shatters.

Structure of lies,
        Collapses.
Personal disaster,
        Who is my master?

What was built by a lie,
        Comes down in a day.
Naked and bare,
        Before Thee alone in despair.

Wasted years,
        It appears.
Just another lie,
        Battle in mind reclaiming soul left behind.

Desperate, alone,
        Tears and pain.
Decades of grief,
        Poison drawn from soul.

My life is a mess,
        Months to digress.
Years to digest,
        Finally at rest.

Nothing left to be taken,
           Nothing more to lose.
Stripped to my core,
           A victim no more.

Part III

Love came down,
           And rescued me.
Passion in action,
           Liberated and free.

New thoughts of my Lover,
           New beauty I see.
Lies are exposed,
           Truth I now see.

Reforming my thoughts,
           Truth about me.
Cleansing of dirt,
           Abuse isn't me.

No longer defined by sin done to me,
           No longer a victim acting from shame.
Pain slowly morphs to joy,
           Regrets are redeemed, I am made clean.

Changing of thoughts,
           Turning to Him, not to shame.
Coming clean to my Love,
           He already knows my new name.

No reason to hide,
           Love bares my soul.
Warmth inside,
           Beauty exposed.

Arms wide open,
> God rescued me.
Freedom has come,
> Not all gentle as supposed.

Shattered are thoughts,
> About who I am.
Truth has brought down,
> Now exposed.

Peace, peace,
> Enters my soul.
Only in Him does healing come,
> Redemption has come.

Battle continues,
> My mind can be slow.
To embrace his truth,
> And just let it be so.

Dawn is breaking,
> Darkness is fleeing.
Alive from the dead,
> Crushed, yet not destroyed.

Walk with a limp,
> Never forget.
He rescued me,
> Setting me free.

Journey

The journey alone,
> Rattled to bone.
I never thought this would be,
> Even my lover can't come with me

Battered and bruised,
> Looking for anyone to travel with me.
No one can walk those places I must go,
> Life sucked out ever so slow.

I thought I would find a father of sorts,
> That's not reality, delusional thought.
The point is alone with God, just me,
> Naked and bare, oh so scared.

Cornered and trapped like a feral cat,
> No escape from my crap.
Alone must go through eye of a needle,
> Stretched so thin breaking of skin.
> Pain leaks out of my soul.

Scorn and shame,
> Broken in pain.
Bloody and stained,
> Mind emptied and lame.

Hiding

Oh hiding what a friend,
You have been.

Covering sin,
Afraid of who I am.

Shame cloaks and covers,
Not wanting discovered.

Comforting pain,
Won't risk again.

Behind protective thoughts,
I won't be caught.

Behind "righteous" acts,
Safety in facts.

Behind spirituality,
Not reality.

Facades so thin,
A veil dingy with sin.

Hide behind "the right words,"
How absurd.

The stench is of death,
Alone in the shame.

There is a Redeemer,
To rescue He came.

No longer alone,
Connected with Him.

No fear of others,
Shame can't smother.

Uncomfortable to be,
Transparent you see.

Awkward and shy,
Step beyond lies.

Judgments no longer,
Can control my thoughts.

Reality demands me to be true,
To who He created me to be.

Frost

Frost that came,
        Soul's cold bane.
Oh the pain,
        White and pure the stain.

Old growth seared,
        Frozen tears.
Dormant times,
        Death's chimes.

Leaves of color,
        Oh the Fall.
The sin of Man,
        God hear my call.

Blown in the Wind,
        Bitter and sweet.
Not even a friend,
        Alone again.

Back to that place,
        Fallen on face.
Desperate for Your Grace,
        No begging in this place.

Walk out this season,
        Cease with reason.
No more treason,
        Stop hiding lesions.

Healing comes,
        Fallow ground.
Tilled and worked,
        Clods busted down.

So Far Away

So far away from You today,
I want to rest in Your arms and stay.

Give myself and all I am,
To You my Lover, my heart is Yours.

I long to know You deep inside,
My mind no longer judging and managing.

No more self-inflicted separation from You,
You long for me to come to You.

Waiting no more to experience You,
I choose today to come to You.

Broken and calling me, I whisper Your name,
No longer want to play a game.

All of me with all of You,
To live today One with You.

Holy Spirit I love You so,
Flow deep within my longing soul.
I don't know how to let the old crap die.

The Truth is pure, the Truth is ugly,
Of who I've been, damage of sin.

Restoration isn't cheap, but it's free,
Connected with You, it's all about You loving me.

I can't make my way without You I see,
Come walk with me, I long for Thee.

Hear my cry, know my heart,
I love You, I love You; today's a fresh start.

Broken Places

Part I

Body breaking down,
        Knocked down.
Stress all around,
        Racing thoughts abound.

Broken places,
        Empty spaces.
Wounded faces,
        Abounding graces.

So weary,
        Tired of dreary.
Broken down,
        Knocked to the ground.

Racing heart,
        Two far apart.
Disconnected and alone,
        Lost in the drone.

Mentally broken,
        No more words spoken.
Emotionally broken,
        Can't trust reality.

What I believed torn down,
        Crumpled on the ground.
Ground to dust,
        Nothing to trust.

Part II – Rest

No longer fear the pain it just is,
        No more squirming to get away.
When does healing come after all's been destroyed,
        Am I just a toy.

What does love look like in broken places,
        Freedom for the anguish no more of me to languish.

Be still my mind, thoughts be kind,
        Self-abuse you are of no use.
You aren't my friend,
        Don't want you anymore.

Be still my heart,
        Be free.
To explore,
        Be more.

Emotions be still no more torture,
        You will not rule my will.

Soul connected with Holy Spirit,
        He is right here.
Nothing to fear,
        Amidst the tears.

Open my arms,
        Embrace Him.
In Him is no harm,
        Don't be alarmed.

Pain will pass,
        Tears won't last.
He is good,
        Stress done and pain is gone.

Rest in Him,
	He is my friend.
So much rattled and shaken.

Keep my focus on Him,
	Rest,
	Rest,
	Rest,
	He has my best.

You Alone

God help, You alone are my hope,
        You alone are my refuge.
You alone are my comfort,
        Yet I desire to receive comfort from another.
I lay that place down before You,
        You are my ultimate comfort.
I lay my desire before You,
        You alone are the warmth and compassion that is
        healing to my soul.
I lay my desire to be heard and known in marriage before You, it is
Yours,
        You alone have known me, seen my sorrows and pain,
        my joy and happiness.
You are my completeness,
        You are my joy and satisfaction.
In You I am known,
        In You I am seen – there is no shame in the past
        anymore, I no longer hide from You.
I run to You,
        I expose myself to You.
I make myself vulnerable to You,
        I choose to turn to You.

24th Wedding Anniversary

Skiff of snow,
      White and clean.
Melts away muddy stain,
      Like years of pain.

I Will Praise You

I will praise You,
> In the midst of tired and torn.

I will praise You,
> Even when broken and worn.

I will praise You,
> In the midst of my storm.

I will praise You,
> Your truth is so sweet.

I will praise You,
> You are my Way.

I will praise You,
> Even in the darkness You still see me.

I will praise You,
> Broken and bruised.

I will praise You,
> In the place of used and abused.

I will praise You,
> You are worthy.

Surrender

I give You everything,
>Though I fight and struggle in that place.
I willingly surrender,
>Giving You all of me in this moment.

I give myself to You,
>All that I am to You I give.

There is no life outside of You,
>Stop the flailing tantrum of pain.
Just give it away to You, really nothing to lose,
>Worth it all to gain You.

No more scapegoat,
>No more tantrums, no more abuse.
Sit in this place,
>Raw, naked, broken with pain.
No more blaming, casting it back at You,
>Your embrace is what I desire.
A touch, a look,
>Cleansing holy fire.
Shed the skin,
>New holy desire.

No more bracing against You,
>Turning, facing You.
I accept Your truth,
>Freedom comes.
No longer about answers,
>It is about a place in Him.
All the unanswered given to Him,
>He touches my pain.
I accept the Truth,
>Cast down the lies.
The fight of the lies,
>Conflicted and torn.

The fight fades away,
        No more abuse, me to Him.
The pain is okay,
        Mine to own.
Give it up to Him,
        I own it, it can just be.
Healing the "be,"
        Sets me free.
A work of the heart,
        Exposure of soul.

Rage Is A Cage

Naked, exposed,
        Falling and flailing.
Pain squirting out,
        Pushed others away.
The effect opposite of heart's desire pushing God out,
        Yet wanting Him in.
All of the pain,
        All of the sin.
Rage is a cage,
        Traps deep within.
The battle that rages,
        Just to give in.
I yield to Him,
        Give Him my sin.
Honest and free,
        Truthful with what I believe about Him.
Pain in the incongruent places, purging the lies,
        The tears I cry.
Redeem the damage of lies,
        Is now my heart's cry.

Naked in Thought

No more whoring mind,
        Perverting the divine.
Not coerced or forced, no more mental divorce,
        Open access between two minds, leaving nothing
        behind.
Naked in thought,
        With the ones I love.
Freely give them,
        All my life.
Passion of thought,
        The inner life.
Out of death and darkest grave,
        Give myself away.
Honesty and light penetrate the darkest night,
        Warm thoughts, dark thought bare before them.

Truth sets free, unlocks caged mind,
        No shame or fear, exposed and free.

Just as I am, no more dishonesty,
        Open and honest lover I'll be.
No shadow or hiding, I humbly expose me,
        Give myself away, to cherish and protect in thoughts
        and mind.
A mind meld willing give to my lover.

Exposure and truth from free choice I give.
Light to expose thoughts and beliefs,
        To explore and be explored.
Realign my thought,
        Renew my mind.
In that place,
        Intimacy divine.

Us

Lover's brown eyes captivating deep pools,
Her kindhearted compassion flows so free.
Hazel eyes igniting kindred fuel,
Shy, nervous happiness drew her you see.

Brunet hair frames beautiful complexion,
Mystical feminine intelligence.
His conformation caught her attention,
Analytical manly confidence.

Revealing red dress caresses her flesh,
She draws vigor from spiritual depths.
Blond and ruddy, a rookie who is fresh,
His fountainhead of life from heaven's breath.

Bodies delightfully woven tightly,
Igniting passion's flame rather brightly.

Wedding Of Our Waters

She is here   I am there

Diverging streams   Conflicted dreams

All of our crap   Close the gap

So we fight   With all our might

Crest the hill   Closer still

Rivers surge   As we converge

All debris   Swept out to sea
Til our distance and wounds are healed

Tough Places

Harsh words spoken,
        Spirits broken.
Eyes once gleaming,
        Now confused meaning.
Always on edge,
        Dangling at ledge.
Threat of leaving,
        Always grieving.
Can we mend,
        Will it ever end?
Just let go,
        See what flows.
Battered and worn,
        Soul forlorn.
Hope lost,
        Restored at great cost.

Dark Heart

Words "domestic violence" strike fear in men's souls.
Not all violence is a physical beating – though all domestic violence bruises the soul.
Not even aware of internal condition or rage, in the moment so out of touch.
Rooted in a stained, damaged heart.
Acting out from a place of own abuse, a dark place of the heart.
Topic fear to broach, society and church ignore.
Uncomfortable, makes us squirm.
Yet honest, open discussion required for healing.
Must willingly go to places of stain in heart and soul for redemption.
Truth is my words caused harm to the ones I love and comes from dark places within.
Cannot deny, it doesn't work and still leaves darkness in my heart.
Not a simple journey, a struggle.
Redemption comes slowly, painfully slow.
Vulnerable and truthful about condition of heart.
Rest comes in truth, words "domestic violence" no longer empowered.
Offer hope by telling the story.

Dark Space

After forty years light flashes in dark places.
Dark space, hidden face.
Safety in shadows a child's mind races.
What have I done where will I hide?
Light displaces dark places in mind.
A dusty dark attic filled full of lies.
Blinding light exposes it all – fear and tears I cried.
Twisting the mind and truth when young.
The beating and terror from abuser's deep rage.
Blocked and suppressed, pain ran silent and deep.
Damage was done, it was sick and deceit.
Quiet and secret, no one to tell a living hell.
In a cage I put myself.
Bound to secrets and lies.
Along comes Grace invading my space.
No hiding, no fear come as I am .
No place for a victim, will I draw near?
Too good to be true, it must be a dream.
No longer the victim, no more self-effort, self-righteousness, or
self-justification.

No more perpetrator, perpetrating my pain on my wife or my kids.
Emotional pain I inflicted on them so hard to explain.
Honest about the sin that's within, light in the darkness casts down
shame.

The wounds on them weren't physical you see.
The wound inflicted were rage, rising up, intimidating,
manipulating, fear.
Could see crushed innocence in their sad eyes.
My actions were different, but results were the same as my
abuser's.
Blind in the dark, until grace and light came.

Each step of the way God asked me if I would go there?
The choice was mine, His love would never be less.

Becomes about finding that place, intimate with Him.
Vulnerable, honest He's not afraid.
Nor is He surprised by the baggage of sin.
He beckons me just as I am.
He invites me to enter in.

Tires

Like a tire,
>It serves it purpose but when balanced the ride is
>smoother.

Like a prophet,
>Balanced with personally seeing Him face to face.

Like a marriage,
>Intimacy and sex.

Like faith and works.

Like love, hope, and faith.

When aligned and balance ride is smoother.

Tire will get you there,
>It wears better and smoother ride when balanced and
>aligned.

Like mercy and justice,
>Father forgive them, have mercy on perpetrator and
>bring justice for me – not mutually exclusive.

She's On A White Horse

Peace in that place.
Embraced in glow of Eden's sunset.
On a white horse.
Softness of golden skin.

Warmth of horse.
Warmth of maiden.
Clothed in His presence.
Intimate with creation and Creator.

Intimate with her lover.
Intimate with her God.
Intimate with creation.

Ran Dry

The well ran dry that day.
Pump and pump as much as you may.
No more tears, free of fear.
No more words they took flight from my soul.

Hollow words making life hard to swallow.
Reality follows.
Don't get lost.
Don't wallow.

Emotions unleashed.
Rabid and mean.
Pent up anger.
Facade so serene.

Pain twists and warps.
Abuse at the surface pussy and gross.
A virus oh shit.
I've lived as its host.

Springing its trap.
Full of stuffed crap.
Secrets are out.
Their power's lost clout.

Choking and drowning in memories so faint.
Mind wants to deny and say it ain't.
Truth says it's true.
That was done to you.

Divides and separates as truth comes to light.
It left a mark even in the dark.
Wound in the soul to be made whole.
Innocence lost, memories with great cost.

Days and weeks where I am tossed.
Sanity lost.
Foggy and murky in dullness of days.
Groggy and sleepy, numbness, coping one more day.

Time goes by in the blink of an eye.
Months pass, pain subsides.
Memories still a splinter in the eye.
No more tears to cry.

Life goes on.
Forgive and walk on.
Let go of the past.
Finally free at last.

A twinge of pain blinks across face.
Time to time memories to embrace.
Glimpses of places and times.
God brings healing and then I'm fine.

No one can share the journey with me.
Others have pain, all have stains.
Each with a struggle, every Man's bane.
Take it to God, don't perpetuate the same.

Safe

Safe is a place,
        Where pain is erased.
Safe is a word,
        Where mind finds solace.
Safe is a touch,
        Where I am embraced.
Safe is a look,
        Where I can get lost.
Safe is a taste,
        Where I can linger without haste.
Safe is warm,
        Refuge in life's' storms.
Safe is a spot,
        Warmth of sunlight melting frost.

Floated Down

The snow floated down,
        Grace covered the ground.
Reflected light,
        In dark of night.
Soft and cold,
        Washing the old.
Made virgin again,
        So let's begin.

All of the crap,
        A bad rap.
Pain of past,
        Gone at last.
Forgiveness resets,
        Relationships past.

Grace covers me,
        Broken and free.
Sin nips at heals,
        Trying to steal.
Don't bury the lies,
        Cry.

Jesus died,
        Now at His side.
Jesus raised,
        God be praised.

There is no try,
        That's why Jesus died.
Enter in grace,
        Gaze at His face.

Collapse in His arms,
        Heart to heart free from harm.

Mercy and grace,
        Opens a space.
A place of embrace,
        To dwell face to face.

Gone

Fully engaged with the three in One.

Just glimpses and tastes,
        Leave starving for more.
Where did He go?
        Why can't I see?
        I know He didn't leave.

Washed Anew

Washed anew,
        No regrets.
Weight lifted,
        Totally free.
Won't be like our first time,
        Will be like never before.
Healthy desire,
        Passion's smoldering fire.
New flames,
        With God's holy breath blown into a blaze.
Two souls become one.
New attachment of souls,
        Bonds of light that distance can't separate.
Not a cord with which to be bound,
        But a bond of light – soul to soul, mate to mate.
Near or far, silent or loved attachment is there,
        Not drawing life but giving life, mine to her and her's to
        me.
As we bask in His light,
        Wrapping us in divine.
Just like in Eden so long ago,
        What was lost has been found, passion flows.
Redeemed and restored,
        The pain is no more.
Longing to be with you like never before!

Peace in Pain

Peace in pain.
Pieces in pain.
Torrents of pain.
Insane pain.

Quiet places finally sooth soul bruises.
Mind at rest passed the test.
Destroyer came with pain.
Empty handed he leaves, I have no more shame.

Propaganda and lists, shallow and empty no quick fix.
Crushed and broken no more to be spoken.
Eyes tell it all, words are small.
Love had been tested and the storm has passed by.
Devourer's appetite must move on, knocking next door.

Each marriage is tested in its own way.
Battle scarred and weary from fight, the fury of hell.
A time to recover, to get well.
Memories come, flashbacks of sorts.
Dreams in the night of battles and passages.
Soul has been rattled.

Let it all go, trust you say.
Easy for you who never passed through this way.
Trials by fire, sleepless nights.
Hold on tight, it's not by might.

In weakness and scars break through heart's prison bars.
Exhausted, consumed no longer room for what has been.
New days and ways to dwell with Him.
Lay it all down, fall to the ground.

Trust

The intellect groans when He asks me to go.
Logic defied will I answer soul's cry.

It makes no sense so I sit on the fence.
War in the head, what's alive and dead?

A moment of courage, a second of trust.
I must rise to the call.

Not about try, but surrender of "I."
An instant of faith and everything changes.

Usually gets harder, not easier as mind wages war.
Thoughts scream this is crazy and hurry close that door.

Faith defies intellect.
Intimacy melts fear.

The warmth of His whispers is what I long to hear.
In that place all melts away, I am safe and at peace in midst of
unknowns.

More to life than reason and intellect.
Back in their place no longer idols fighting with Him.

Proof of my love in entering His place.
At risk of losing all, outcome unknown.
Trust is a must that defies the mind.
Trust — issue of the heart.

Breaking Free

The beautiful damsel, Colleen is her name,
           Breaking free, she is untamed.
Out of the darkness into the light,
           Worshipping God in deepest of night.

Longing of heart still to be known,
           So much beauty yet to be shown.
Scarred and abuse in most hurtful of ways,
           Redemption shall come with no more delay.

Years of heartache restored,
           No longer ignored.
Words were spoken,
           Power's been broken.

Through the heart of her lover,
           Wounds given now he will cover.
Tears cried from verbal abuse,
           Anoints with salve til her soul's completely infused.

Stretching her wings he encourages her flight,
           Soar so high to beautiful height.
Gracefully floating on his passionate thermals,
           Union of two always eternal.

Souls are tied, no more divide,
           Salvation has come, now we abide.
Hearts exchanged marriage transformed,
           New union formed.

Pursuit

Hot on the trail,
      Mission mustn't fail.
My maiden is gone,
      Changed to a knight from a pawn.

She's been taken away,
      Imprisoned today.
Mount my stead,
      Light armor need speed.

Hour by hour closing the gap,
      Lightening, thunder clap.
The storm has been raging,
      I awoke from my raving.

To battle I go to rescue my love,
      An innocent dove.
Dash into the fray,
      My maiden to save.

Surprised my enemy, rushed into his camp,
      Blade drawn and snuffed out his lamp.
Knight and maiden riding side by side,
      God is our guide.

Back to the castle the feast can begin,
      A toast to our story now free from sin.
Our new life,
      As husband and wife.

Training and Meetings

Webinar occurs afar,
      Might as well be Mars.
Revenue meters,
      Heads teeter.
Room is hot,
      We need some cots.
Flags in corner,
      Stuck in meeting, just a mourner.
Makes a long day,
      Mind becomes gooey clay.
Boring as hell,
      Ring the recess bell.
More barriers to do my job,
      All the joy has been robbed.
Lost sight of what we do,
      Just a bunch of bureaucrats without a clue.
What took a day now takes weeks,
      Take it and shove it down their beaks.
Looks good on paper,
      When it doesn't work turns into a caper.
It's about building empires,
      Won't tell the truth, just a liar.
Power and control follow their edict,
      This won't end well I predict.
All the words seem so wise,
      Seals their fate, their demise.
Pendulum swings to the extreme,
      HQ is giddy they create the teams.
Players are picked because they say yes,
      Way to advance so expect nothing less.
Integrity left and they didn't know,
      Our external customers will halt our show.
No longer give feedback, won't tickle their ears,
      Overreaction out of their fears.

It will get ugly, a crisis will cure,
> Don't waste a manipulated crisis with all its allure.

Inevitable train wreck,
> Disengaged, will be interesting to watch oh what the
> heck.

From beginning of time cycle repeats,
> When it crashes their offspring they'll eat.

Photography

Moments captured in time with one click.
Emotions of life – a birth, wedding, or death.
Can go back in time removing each brick.
Family and love with each baited breath.

Fade to black and white memories purged.
Vivid and bright at first break of dawn's light.
Two tones closer to funeral dirge.
Colors ignite glorious joy each night.

Old medium is transparent film faded.
New medium consists of zeros and ones.
Old memories diluted and jaded.
New memories fresh, naively begun.

Captured the joy when memories fade.
Coloring mind with love potently made.

Life Alone

Not created to live life alone,
        There's more to life than a telephone.
Friends are essential nourishment to soul,
        Without others in life a rather large hole.
Not just a passing "hi how are you,"
        A breaking of bread, hearty relational stew.
Community is lacking between those beside,
        So much easier to pretend and just hide.
Begins with a risk,
        Be ready, emotionally frisked.
If I am seen,
        What will that mean?
Ambivalent desires of heart,
        Red Sea must part.
Death to choice of isolation,
        Soul no longer rationed.
To be valued and warm,
        Found port in the storm.
Accepted and safe,
        Touched and known.
Alive and renewed,
        No longer subdued.

Hotels

The number of nights spent in hotels.
Is my job really worth this type of hell?
Five months here, eleven months there.
Reality is managers don't care.

Missed out on family so much.
Guilt, hardship and such.
In some ways got us to a point.
Where could confront dysfunction, relationally out of joint.

The rooms look the same.
Managers and workers all knew my name.
Sometimes when gone so many weeks.
When wake up must reorient, memory freaks.

Stress of the job, responsibility great.
Multimillion dollar projects ultimately feel the heat.
Review the designs and I just pine.
Comments ignored, they pretend it's just fine.

They hide in their cubicles, deep in their holes.
Learn on the fly, project managers cry.
All of the "fixes" that I must do.
Escalates costs, the dollars just flew.

Trip test equipment that's what I do.
Before do that must program the network to talk to the RTU.
Months of my time doing design work that's not mine.
Looking at monitor, won't get put in service until I say fine.

The groans in the room when I say commissioning takes one year.
They magically think wave a wand and it all just appears.
Construction schedules change and cost escalates.
Organization can't plan, just jerkily sputters and hesitates.

They wonder why I'm pissed.
It effects my family I miss.
They don't miss birthdays.
Or anniversaries, their families don't pay.

Walls of hotel all are white.
Same types of furniture each night.
Little bottles of shampoo.
And conditioner too.

Don't know if coming or going.
Lots of windshield time I'm doing.
More time at hotel than at home.
My soul lets out a sorrowful groan.

Marriages often fail in this field.
Such a struggle, resolve must be steeled.
How many fights caused by absence of night?
Wife all alone, legitimate gripes.

Sunrise

Dark blue with blob of mauve,
        Daubed the horizon.

Fingers of light reach out from the edge,
        Creasing the sky, wonder to eye.
Doesn't last long as sun bursts above the ledge,
        The day has begun, resting is done.

Molly and I walk in the field,
        She is happy to be with just me.
She jumps up with joy, she's big and she's stout,
        Ready to run her day has begun.

Black and white fur pent full of energy,
        She sits to be rubbed, a type of synergy.
She sniffs and she pulls on leash life to the full,
        Steady my mind before work and its bind.

Fifteen minutes is all that it takes,
        The half mile walk a piece of cake.
Quiet and still world not awake,
        Horses all sleeping under Molly's safe keeping.

Clutter

The clutter of the day.
Mind scattered and frayed.
Quiet the soul, grounded at rest.
Thoughts buzz around, life sucking pests.

Journey

The journey more than expected.
Rawness of passages.
Through desert places.
Dry, dusty, parched and blazing hot during day.
Brutally cold at night.
Wander alone in a passage that can only make alone.
Moments of oasis and refreshing then push on.
Terrain begins to change subtly.
Is it the internal terrain?
What was meant to crush turned in time.
Look at the dark night of soul in different light.
What could have been another tragic ending,
Instead a redemption story.
No quick fixes.
An individual journey but not meant to walk solo.
Only in safe community does landscape change.
When shame loses grip and able to tell story without flinching or
cringing others find hope.
Hope in just being able to say to another "I know."
They can tell if truly walked it out and comfort that brings.
Community able to call "bullshit" when put on veneer.
Exposure brings healing, no more secrets.
Peace comes with each exposure, as willingly embrace reality of
who I am and what I have or haven't done.
Failures no longer have a hold.
Each day new hope.

Internal Places

Not solid internal places.
Heart broken.
Internal hypocritical faces.
Eternal love can't fill place of self-validating love.
When words spoken more distance.

When solid within distance is no longer focus.
"Confront" him is lost into a place of realizing I don't need to get
in his face.
My "offensives" say more about who I judge myself to be, not
about others response to me.
Fighting with me about "offensive" and "confronting" when that is
a projection of protection.

I have freedom.
To see.
That my anxiety,
From not having place of solid, silenced love.
Always looking for external love.
When issue is being peaceful and loving internally.
I strike out when external love is distant.
Stirs up my lack of internal love.
The truth is uncomfortable, painful.

Pain in reality.

Lonely and isolated.
Withdraw to inward space.
Vulnerability trampled on.

Angry at myself not solid enough to be true and congruent.
Angry I should have known better – shame.
Touched that place between us.
Erupts violently, unpredictably like volcano

So much molten bitterness, anger.
Seething beneath surface.
One false step, one missed word.
Out it oozes scorching the souls it touches.

Igniting fires of already burned land.
A type of hell, burning and re-burning.
No time to heal.
Just more charring of soul.

If solid internally would be like Teflon™.
It wouldn't stick or hurt.
There would be no scar.
If loved myself instead of looking to others.

Herd of Deer

Breaking of dawn.
A herd of deer.
Take a moment.
They bound away.

Leaving me like I had seen ghosts.
Blending into surroundings in dim light.
A second to soak it in.
I ponder beauty and grace as they disappear.

An awesome way to start the day.
Changes focus to beauty in the midst of my tears.
Pain of relationship exchanged for a moment in beauty of creation.
A more solid self I become drinking life in.

Gift of life.
God is good.
He knows what speaks to me.
Even when I don't in the moment.

As reflect on moment it pulls me out of pain.
To see beauty of His creation.
Could be a sunrise or sunset, could be an animal.
Could be lover's nude body and soul.

Friends from Afar

Friends from afar.
Left in rental car.
Fly away.
To home today.

A brief reprieve.
Still we grieve.
Laughter and joy had.
We were glad.

By tonight be on coast.
Time we had vaporous, a ghost.
A glimpse again.
Relationships bane.

Cycles

Places of pain.
What to do with painful experiences?
Experience that repeats despite awareness.
Broken in that place.
Damages relationship.
A panicky, nervousness inside.
Ready to bolt before even aware.
Move to that solid, grounded internal place.
Must learn to love myself in those places before I can effectively love another.
Love your neighbor as yourself.
The problem is I am loving my neighbor as I love myself.
I don't like what the truth of that reveals about me.

Good to Me

God is good to me.
He is with me like the breeze brushing my face.
Unseen but felt, undeniable.
When I fail He is there.
When I sin He holds me close.
When I am sinned against he presses closer.
He is always gracious and forgiving.
He is not like me, He doesn't struggle with forgiving when
wronged.
He always accepts me, even when I reject myself He presses in.
He longs for me to come and enter in with Him.
He never tires of my tears or heartaches.
He never tires of hearing my self-inflicted heartache.
He overlooks the folly of my ways.
He redeems the years I have wasted.
I see the folly of wasted years, bullheadedness.
Arrogant, thinking I'm wise.
My wisdom was folly and acknowledge my folly.
He is good and will bring restoration to all the harm I have caused.
He is good to me.

Confluence

Boundaries and frontiers.
Must surrender and overcome fears.
A land watered by tears.
Full of naysayers and jeers.

Stand alone in that place.
Directing three that merge in that space.
Conductor as commotion and collisions occurs.
Violent at times needing to use spurs.

Frothing emotions.
Demotions and promotions.
Can only be on frontier, wild and free.
Breaking and making buckling knees.

Fear in moment will I stand or flee?
Who will I be?
Debris fills the center as conductor directs.
He is calm in the storm, chaos has no effect.
Over the edge plunges beliefs.
Doctrines ejected what a relief.
Carried away to places can't see.
What's been bound inside released and who will I be.

Strong find they're weak.
Weak find they're strong.
All courage has leaked.
Only a few, not a willing throng.

Collision of dreams.
What does it mean?
Must let them go.
Embrace currents flow.

Relationships changed.
Now foreign and strange.
Rearranged lives.
Filled with new drive.

Swept away on frontier.
Boundaries disappeared.
Radical change.
No longer estranged.

Head in His Mane

Bury head in His mane.
Sorrow and grief extracted.
Drawn from the soul.
Let tears and weeping flow.
The stuck sorrow extracted.

Voice Raise

How can I love You in a meaningful way to You? In the midst of
the weirdness, worship Him anyway – praise Him for His
goodness.

In His presence is no fear,
   My love towards Him hear.
Fiery love in holy place,
   His joyous face.

Come up to Him,
   Behind is dim.
Weights lift,
   Float and drift.

Chains broken,
   Healing spoken.
Set free,
   Just agree.

In river of Light float,
   Get out of boat.
Drink in deep,
   Wake up from sleep.

Renewed and refreshed,
   With Him meshed.
Words of praise,
   My voice raise.

Palm Sunday 2015

A change of mind.
True repentance I find.
You are kind.
Your love isn't blind.

Your love sees all.
Even in ugliness You beckon and call.
Inviting me today.
Your forgiveness display.

Naked and bare.
Do not despair.
He sees.
He touches me.

Embarrassed and shameful.
He embraces me and all that is painful.
All I have suffered.
He flips for His good, no need to buffer.

Second Day – Tomb 2015

As Church celebrates Easter tomorrow, today is the day of the
tomb.
New Paradigm on Easter, on His love for me.
Adam's choice in the Garden, that moment.
Open rebellion, willful choice to eat the fruit.
Was it possible that he wasn't solid internally just prior?
That what Eve reflected back to him validated him more than God?
The brokenness of choices, exposure.
The Fall exposed that place in Adam's heart.
The weak place he wasn't solid internally with God.
Just watch it all unfold.
How could the serpent know?
Had the serpent been watching and observing?
Spying on them, looking for weak place?
He divided and conquered, shrewdly.
So much I don't understand.

The frailty of Man.
In all the beauty and glory, the frailty.
Always thought of Adam as some super hero, Superman.
Yet, he was a man, no different than I.
I fall to the scheme myself, over and over.
The place of individual and relationship.
Just like Adam I have relationship available with God.
Yet look to woman to reflect back to me worth and value.
A place of attack from the enemy, to go after weakness there.
Vulnerable place, unprotected place of longing to be validated.
What would it have looked like for Adam to refuse the offer?
Where would Adam have had to have been internally to refuse?
Tested in same way Adam was.
Why is my response always frail, out of fear – not from a solid
internal place?
Looking for validation in wrong places.
Creates anxiety, fear, abandonment, rejection , shame.
Yet like a dog to its vomit find myself in the cycle – looking for
validation, love, and acceptance in wrong places.

To be free of it.
To embrace failing with arms open wide – beauty in the fail, fall,
and recovery.
Beauty of redemption, of Jesus.
He is beautiful.
To gaze upon Him.
Will I get an opportunity before the other side?
Not just an image in my mind, but a real encounter.
What would his voice sound like?
What color are His hair and eyes?
What would He wear?
Would I be able to embrace Him?
What does His smile look like?
Could I bear to look at Him in the eyes?
Could I take Him seeing into all of me – good, bad, ugly, sin?

Would He tell me what's on His heart?
Would one touch heal all my broken places?
What would just being in His presence be like?
I would be changed in an encounter with Him.
Reconciliation of Adam with Jesus – Jesus as second Adam.
Jesus is familiar with all my frailties, yet without sin.
He carried all my iniquities, He knows my sins.
Would He find me interesting?
What would we talk about?

Easter 2015

Easter dresses, three piece suits.
Heart so broken, voice is mute.
Lonely inside so far apart.
Painful to be together, no place to start.

Separate lives in separate places.
Look but don't touch expression on faces.
Just need to leave, stop pretending.
Hope has faded, nor more heart rending.

So much pain, can't communicate.
Too much experienced, can sense the hate.
Emptiness without forgiveness, so what's the point?
So damaged and out of joint.

Longing to be desired for who I am.
No reconciliation, repair attempts now a sham.
In the tomb such a long time.
Ready to end it, wasted my prime.
Dark thoughts are in my mind.
I can't remember happy times?
Just the fights and struggle to stay together.
Once thought it would be forever.

My Easter Act of Worship

In the midst of my pain I choose to worship You.
In the midst of my disappointment I choose to worship You.
You gather my tears, they are precious to You
My broken heart an act of worship to You.

Even though I don't feel You, I believe You care for me.
When I am hopeless, You are faithful to me.
My heart rages when rejected and You care.
You understand me when I don't even understand myself.

When I can't love myself You love me.
When my pain blinds me, consumes me, You don't abandon me.
When I am lonely You see me.
When I long to be touched You reach for me.

I wish I could feel Your physical touch.
I wish I could hear your audible voice, tender toward me.
I wish You could wipe my tears.
I wish I could feel You hold me tightly and not let go.

My soul bleeds and You see.
My heart aches and You feel.
My mind swirls and You know
My emotions cycle and You understand.

You know my sorrow.
You know my emptiness.
You know my longings.
You are my only Hope of redemption, reconciliation – making
things right.

Alone

Hurt and anger.
Pain of being alone.
Pain of advances rejected.
Depression.

Ready to give up.
Tired of the struggle.
Tired of the fight.
I am spent, don't have the energy anymore.

Sorrow and grief.
What could have been now lost.
Wasted years and wasted life.
All to be alone, lonely.

A blackness in heart and soul.
The vortex sucks me in.
I'm caught in its grip.
And to that place I must go.

Lonely and alone.
Deep despair and pain.
Meaning I'm not worth it.
Not worthy of being loved.

That is the pain.
Sharp slap of rejection.
A familiar place.
Can't get free.

Where is healing?
Where is redemption?
Where is hope?
Where is love?

Just more tears.
Sorrow consumes.
Pain with each fail.
Alone.

Help

Ignored, project, scapegoat.
Not seen, not known.
In broken place she will not come and sit with me.
That place is offensive to her.

Anger and rage as see her but won't enter in.
Distance, emptiness, and pain.
Left alone in place of sorrow.
She assumes there will always be tomorrow.

If "he" would deal with "his" shit then "she" would feel better.
When she could enter into relationship and be known.
Doesn't work that way.
If won't enter into place of deepest pain won't be able to enter in
deepest place of intimacy.

The two are spiritually linked.
How much is it about him?
How much of it is about her?
He's always made the bad guy, always "doing it" wrong.

Perhaps the truth is it is just life?
What is he going to do with it?
What is she going to do with it?
Can pull together or push apart.

A question of the mind?
A question of the heart?
A question of will he let go of his relationship with "his" past?
A question of will she let go of her relationship with "his" past?

He puts himself in a mold.
Formed in their many years.
He can't get out.
Trapped inside.

Trapped in the past.
Struggle to get free.
Battle for integrity and congruence.
A hard fought inner peace.

When does relief come?
When does peace settle within?
When does sleep return?
When does hope rise up?

Weary and forsaken.
Rattled and shaken.
Battered and scarred.
Soul bleeding, mind crippled, emotions broken.

Carnage of disaster.
People watch the spectacular crash in slow motion.
A cringe in the soul, stopping the heart momentarily.
Deep gasps of breath as the chaos stops, just broken mess revealed.

Everything stops.
Am I alive?
Where is she?
Is she alive?

Grogginess of trauma.
Slowly awaken.
What is missing from soul?
What parts of me have been lost?

What parts of her have been lost?
What parts of us have been lost?
Will we ever recover?
Or is this the end?

Where is redemption?
Where is reconciliation?
Where is forgiveness?
Where is healing?
Where is love?

God where is Your help?
I cry out to You – HELP
Does this ever change?
I need Your hope!

Transitions

My world shifts.
Soul sifted.
Motives exposed.
Thoughts deposed.

Heart is raw.
Didn't like what I saw.
Need to change.
Became estranged.

Split apart.
Inward battle for my heart.
Integrity calls.
Incongruence falls.

Deep within.
Away from din.
Battle rages.
No sages.

Loud silence,
Takes up residence.
Who am I?
Old ways say good-bye.

Peace settles in thoughts.
No longer caught.
From deep inside,
I learn to abide.

Labor Pains

Distractions and contractions.
Labor pains in action.
Blood and water.
Life poured out on blotter.

He's the keeper.
Wake up sleeper.
Life to live.
Beauty to give.

Waves of life.
Let go of strife.
Wade out in surf.
Walk barefoot on loamy turf.

Ebb and flow.
His mercies show.
Where can I go?
That He won't know?

In depth of despair.
He still cares.
In height of ecstasy.
He always sees.

Crowns

Crowns of glory,
        Changes story.
Redemption's love,
        Falls as a dove.

His crown is weighty,
        About His brow.
His Kingly state,
        His beauty wows.

Depths of eyes,
        Plows deep inside.
Beauty exposed,
        Soil turned, no longer closed.

Second Day

That place between, each must face.
That personal hell each must embrace.
He plunged into Hell.
He went before me, saw my cell.

With me in mind He took the key.
Knowing what would liberate me.
In those days between one and three.
He boldly walked through the fire to set me free.

Rattle and shake hell's dark gates.
Redeeming me from torturous fate.
When I'm alone comfort is found.
He reached down, grace abounds.

Chains of the mind.
Thoughts so unkind.
Comforting touch brushed away tears.
Redemption of time and wasted years

Head On My Chest

Her head on my chest,
       The warmth of her breath.
Entwining of flesh,
       Complete rest.

Peace in our souls,
       Our spirits caress.
Emotionally seen,
       Mentally known.

Depth from within,
       Exposure of self.
No demands put on my lover,
       No projection of one on another.

True vulnerability discovered,
       Words have new meanings.
Place in context of believing,
       Expressions of me, no longer hide or flee.

A journey within had to begin,
       Fruit of that labor.
Intimacy and longing truly discovered,
       Solid within, the place to begin.

It's taken years,
       Confrontation of fears.
Subject to jeers,
       Overcome and draw near.

Spring 2015 at the Ranch

Spring rain finally came,
       Washing away the long Winter's shame.
Grime and decay,
       Cloudy and gray.

Blossoms and blooms,
       Bursts from their tombs.
Hope abounds,
       New life found.

In the struggle to thrive,
       Thankful to be alive.
Internal victorious win,
       Joy welling up deep within.

Ride It Out

The process sucks,
        Seem so stuck.
Don't need to fight it,
        Don't need to buck.
Embrace the wave,
        Ride it out to sandy shore to be restored.

Today

Hope rising, breaking dawn.
Soft colors paint the sky.
Pinks and blues, fingers of dawns light piercing the sky.
Softness floods darkness of soul.
A new day, a new canvas.
Can I express my gratefulness for another day?
Stillness at dawn, hush on soul.
Engaged in moment.
Don't lose engagement as day progresses.
Recall moment as first rays illuminate the sky.
Brings thankfulness to lips.
Chill of dawn soon to be erased as sun rises.
Warmth washes through me.
Forgetting yesterday – successes and failures.
Today is a new day.
A day for hope and love to be expressed.

New Ways

Intertwined in soul, spirit, and mind.
Emotions flood my being.
Riskiness to bare all.
Return to days before the Fall.

Walls are down, doors wide open.
Invited in to delight again.
Each year requires more growth of me.
Longing for deeper intimacy.

Confronting self and who I've been.
A fierce battle deep within.
Exposed to core, all the ugly gore.
Time of shipwreck, exhausted on the shore.

All seemed lost.
Buried deep in permafrost.
Spring thaws the earth.
Seeds from death, new birth.

Hope begins to rise.
Feelings long forgotten cries.
New ways from depth inside.
No longer want to hide.

Hope Rises

Hope rises,
Resurrection of soul.
Joy surprises,
As made whole.

Walk with a limp,
Never forget.
Observant know the gimp,
Forgiveness unbinds regrets.

Hope rises,
Joy surprises.

Notes

ABOUT THE AUTHOR

Brian and his wife, along with their three children, reside on the western edge of Nebraska. From their small farm they have a distant view of Laramie Peak in Wyoming. They have lived in Western Nebraska for the past 27 years.

Among Brian's eclectic interests are Border Collies, Australian Shepherds and herding dogs; photography; writing; and teaching. He has a degree in mechanical engineering.

You can see more of Brian's writings at http://westernnebraskapoet.blogspot.com.

www.ingramcontent.com/pod-product-compliance
Lightning Source LLC
Chambersburg PA
CBHW071819020426
42331CB00007B/1543